MW01109626

A NEW
NORMAL

a journey from loss to joy

DR. JIM MANN
CHRISTINE MANN

AMBASSADOR INTERNATIONAL
GREENVILLE, SOUTH CAROLINA & BELFAST, NORTHERN IRELAND

www.ambassador-international.com

A New Normal
A Journey from Loss to Joy

Printed in the United States of America

ISBN: 9781935507871

Cover Design & Page Layout by Matthew Mulder and David Siglin
Author Photo by Carol Carter

AMBASSADOR INTERNATIONAL
Emerald House
427 Wade Hampton Blvd.
Greenville, SC 29609, USA
www.ambassador-international.com

AMBASSADOR BOOKS
The Mount
2 Woodstock Link
Belfast, BT6 8DD, Northern Ireland, UK
www.ambassador-international.com

The colophon is a trademark of Ambassador

Dedication

For Mom —
Servata fines cineri, soli de gloria

Memorial Page

Place a picture
of the loved one here.

Contents

Foreword 9

Preface 11

"Broken" 15

Imago Dei 18

Be Imitators of God 20

Helplessness 22

A New Normal 24

The Master Weaver 26

Schadenfreude 29

Psalm 126 31

Fairness Doctrine 33

Demons 35

Treasure 37

Mother 39

Remember 41

Shine 43

Shaded Gray 45

Shadow of Death 47

Florilegium 50

Absurdity 53

Blessed 56

The Bell Tolls 59

In Vain? 61

Childlike Prayer 64

Strong as Death 66

This Shall Be a Sign? 70

Trumped 75

Praises 78

Emotional Lottery 80
Thy Will Be Done 82
Get on with Life 86
On Heaven 89
On Eternity 92
Crossing the Bar 96
Ich Glaube an Gott 99
Sorrow, Joy, and Hope 102
Mom's Birthday 105
On Love 108
Crash 110
In 112
The Setting Sun 114
Scars 117
Final Thoughts 120
Afterword 126

Foreword

THE TRUTH IS SIMPLE; DEATH is a transition. It is a transition not just for those who move from Earth to Heaven but also for those who live on. Death challenges us like nothing else, that is why Hebrews 2:14 says Jesus came to deliver us who were subject to the fear of death. Death demands of our faith; it makes us answer the questions: Do we believe in the face of what we see? Do we believe in the face of what we feel?

Dr. Jim Mann confronts these questions and others head-on. Jim takes us on his personal journey as he walks through the Valley of the Shadow of Death. His honesty and transparency are refreshing. We see what he sees and feel what he feels but, most importantly, we learn what he learned. This book gives you practical ways to master the moments of grief, to begin to embrace God and wrap yourself in the truth of His Word. The insights are powerful yet simple, they provide the first steps to fulfill 1 Corinthians 15:55, "O death where, where is thy sting?" and Romans 8:38 and 39, "For I am persuaded, that neither death, nor life…shall be able to separate us from the love of God, which is in Christ Jesus our Lord".

Jim has done a great job. I encourage you to start the journey today.

—Pastor Gerald Brooks, D.D.
Grace Outreach Center
Plano, TX

Preface

My mother died suddenly several years ago. The Lord was gracious and merciful to walk me through the grieving process. This little book you are reading was an important part of my healing.

I was wholly unprepared for her death. Until that time, I had little acquaintance with sorrow. My grandparents' deaths at very old ages were really the only "grief" I had experienced. My childhood had been like an episode of *Leave it to Beaver* or the *Cosby Show*. I'd been afforded a great education, married my college sweetheart, had my dream job, had two wonderful children . . . nothing in life had prepared me for grief.

Then, at the age of 64, my mom got sick. After a few weeks in the hospital, she looked like she was on the road to recovery. Sitting at work one day I got a call. "You need to get here quick—I can't wake your mother up."

I never had intentions of making these pages public. They represent my fears, doubts, pain, and general angst during this time in my life—not the public image I normally present. I'm not convinced King David would have "published" some of his psalms, either. But as I shared my musings with my wife, then my father, and others going through similar "dark nights of the soul," we discovered them to be helpful.

I'm a pastor. I spent years in seminary. But I never learned much about helping people through grief. Of course, this is crazy; grief will touch us all at one point or another—guaranteed. Yet none of us is prepared. And the shepherds who have the task of walking people through grief are likewise unprepared.

I have since learned a lot about grief. We will all experience grief at the death of a loved one. But grief also comes when a marriage doesn't last. Grief comes when we lose a job. Grief comes when we move. We even experience grief when we lose a beloved pet. And most of us are not prepared for the grieving process.

This is where I found myself several years ago. Not knowing what to do or where to turn, I felt led by the Lord to start journaling my thoughts. I read a few helpful books on grief: Nicholas Wolterstorff's beautiful *Lament for a Son*[1] and Henri Nouwen's *A Letter of Consolation*.[2] I had as a background C. S. Lewis's *The Problem of Pain*[3] and Philip Yancey's *Disappointment with God*.[4] But mostly I read the Scriptures. Cathartically, I began to interact with these and work my way through the haze.

As I mentioned, God's grace and mercy sustained me through the process, and I believe I have emerged a better person and a stronger Christian.

If you bought this journal or were given it by a friend, there's probably a reason. My heart goes out to you in this difficult time. You need to know some things about your grief that will help you heal: grief is natural and normal—a part of life; therefore, you shouldn't avoid it. Don't pretend your sorrow is not there or try to hide your tears. I encourage you to embrace the grief you are facing—analyze it, pray through it, participate in the process, let God heal the wounds naturally.

I have discovered that all grief is different, just as each of us has been created differently by God. That means that you and I won't deal with grief in exactly the same way. Well-meaning advice that

1.   Nicholas Wolterstorff, *Lament for a Son* (Grand Rapids: William B. Eerdmans, 1987).
2.   Henri J. M. Nouwen, *A Letter of Consolation* (San Francisco: HarperSan-Francisco, 1982).
3.   C. S. Lewis, *The Problem of Pain: How Human Suffering Raises Almost Intolerable Intellectual Problems* (New York: Collier Books, MacMillan Publishing House, 1962).
4.   Phillip Yancey, *Disappointment with God: Three Questions No One Asks Aloud* (Grand Rapids: Zondervan, 1988).

has been helpful to others may not help you. In the same way, the timetable for your grieving will be yours and no one else's. So don't rush the process, and don't let others rush you either. It is *your* loss, so this is between you and the Lord.

Finally, it's your grief you must deal with. God will meet you there—it's a promise. It is said of the Lord Jesus, "Surely he took up our pain and bore our suffering" so do what you need to do to work through it *with Him* (Isaiah 53:4a NIV).

In the future, you may be called upon to help others. But you can't do anything for them if healing does not first take place in you.

"Now may the Lord of peace himself give you peace at all times and in every way. The Lord be with all of you."
—2 Thessalonians 3:16 (NIV)

"Broken"

from Psalm 42
A Lament

Why are You far off?
Why do You seem to hide
While my enemies hunt me
And prosper in pride?

Still Your mercy sweeps
Over me like a flood.
Though I'm broken,
I will yet praise my God.
Oh, Your mercy rolls over me,
And I will yet praise You.

My tears are my food;
Why downcast my soul?
When can I meet You
And give You control?

Deep calls to deep,
My soul is revived.
My pain is starting to leave,
And I will yet praise my God.

The water is rising,
Your Spirit is falling
Your love in the day
Your song in the night

A prayer to the God of my life.
And Your mercy sweeps over me
Like a flood.
Though I am broken, I will yet
Praise my God.

READ PSALM 42 AND WRITE your own lament to God. Be honest with Him, freely cry out to Him, and pray honestly, openly presenting your questions to Him. Before you finish, make sure you remind yourself of God's nature (42:8) and praise Him.

_____

_____

_____

_____

_____

_____

_____

_____

_____

_____

_____

_____

_____

_____

_____

_____

_____

Imago Dei

MOM WAS AN ICON. THE Scriptures tell us that she was formed in God's image—the *Imago Dei*—His icon. But she was more than just a silhouette of God's image; she really looked like Him. She laughed and smiled like Him. Is this why it's so hard for me? Has part of God been laid in the ground with her? Has His image been marred, forever changed? Not the all-knowing, all-powerful part of God, but that part that is joyful, hopeful.

Of course, there is the resurrection to look forward to, but that does not bring Mom back in the now. She's gone, as is my joy.

Yes, I think a part of God was laid in that grave, the part that has a twinkle in the eye. The twinkle has been replaced by a tear. A sorrowful, suffering God—that is the God with whom I fellowship today. I will again be acquainted with the God of joy. When, I don't know. But it will be a wonderful reunion. I will again be acquainted with the icon of God that is and was Jane Mann. It too will be a wonderful reunion.

RECALL YOUR LOVED ONE AND his/her impact on your life. Name at least one physical attribute that is etched into your mind. What do you most look forward to in your reunion with the Lord? With your loved one?

_____

_____

_____

_____

_____

_____

Be Imitators of God

*"He was despised and rejected by men; a man of sorrows, and
acquainted with grief; and as one from whom men hide their faces he
was despised, and we esteemed him not."*
—Isaiah 53:3 (ESV)

TODAY, I AM MORE LIKE Jesus. By that, I refer to Isaiah's description of Him as "a man of sorrows." That phrase describes me too. I strive daily for Jesus' character traits . . . but not this one. This is a characteristic of the Lord to which I wish I could not relate.

READ ISAIAH 53. EXPLAIN HOW you can now identify with the "man of sorrows." How does this help you in your grief?

_____

_____

_____

_____

_____

_____

_____

_____

_____

_____

_____

_____

_____

Helplessness

THE PARAMEDIC'S CLINICAL YET NOT unfeeling statement haunts me: "She didn't make it." *Make what?! You mean she died?* It was an accurate diagnosis. Life had left her body as she lay resting in bed.

Faith, I need faith! I will pray like the godly men of old, the men of faith. She will wake up. We will give God glory as we watch Him raise the dead!

How do those Bible stories go? I can't remember. So I try it my own way. Through tears, I cry out to God. *Please, Lord, raise her up!*

No one is in the room with me, but I would not have cared if they were.

Faith. I need more faith! I pray with words. I pray in the Spirit. I pray with sobs and unintelligible groanings. *Mom is still sleeping. Wake up, O sleeper! Wake up, daughter!*

Helpless.

READ JOHN 11:1–44. HOW IS your faith being stretched during this time? Are you feeling helpless? What questions will you ask of God when you meet Him face to face?

_____

_____

_____

_____

_____

_____

_____

_____

A New Normal

A NEW NORMAL. THAT'S WHAT a friend told me we would come to know over time. Life moves on. Kids start school and sports. Sunday service nears. But I'm not normal—not yet.

I think about what this new normality will be like at Halloween—Mom's birthday. I think about Thanksgiving, Christmas, Easter. How will I preach on Mother's Day? A new normality, I guess.

But I don't look forward to it. It will just seem wrong. The family will be together, but not all of us.

Someone once said we are like stones in a bucket of water. When the stone that is our life is removed, water fills the void, and no hole is left. Life goes on as "normal"—a new normal—as if the stone were never there.

Whoever said that never lost a mother.

DEFINE "A NEW NORMAL" FOR your life. What are your feelings as you look toward the coming year? Share your feelings with the Lord: your fears, joys, anxieties, and sorrows. Before you finish, lay each of these at the foot of the cross in prayer.

_____

_____

_____

_____

_____

_____

_____

_____

_____

_____

_____

_____

_____

_____

_____

_____

_____

_____

_____

_____

_____

_____

_____

_____

_____

_____

_____

_____

_____

_____

_____

_____

_____

_____

_____

_____

The Master Weaver

PATHOS IS WHAT I'M EXPERIENCING. Passion. Raw emotion. And one of those emotions is anger. But I'm not angry with God. This is somewhat surprising because I thought I would be. Rather, I'm angry with sin. I'm angry with the demonic enemy, death.

I have never looked at God as a dealer in death. Death was never *His* plan but an aberration to His plan. It was the unfortunate, demonic result of *our* plan that brought death.

A well-meaning but shortsighted friend gave our family a condolence card at Mom's death. On it was a poem called "The Master Weaver." God, as the Master Weaver, is in the process of weaving a beautiful tapestry that is you and me. Of course, we, being the subjects of His work, cannot see the pattern. Only the Master Weaver can do that. And from time to time, the Master Weaver loads the shuttle with a dark strand of pain and grief. Again, as the subjects, we must not question, but trust. For in the end, if we persevere, we will see God's beautiful design, and He will receive glory.

So, "My son, the tapestry of your life is shaping up nicely. Now, I will kill your mother to add character to the design"?

I do not know this weaver. If I did, he would receive the full load of my anger. What's more, I do not want to know him! In my mind, such capriciousness is found only in God's enemy. He is the one who sneaks in and sows tares (see Matthew 13:25). He is the one waiting in the tall grass ready to pounce (see 1 Peter 5:8). He is the one who steals, kills, and destroys (see John 10:10). That is not God's doing.

When the disciples grappled with this same question in John 9, their question to Jesus about the man born blind was, Why did God do this to him? Why did the Master Weaver load his shuttle with blindness? Jesus' answer is astonishingly simple: God did not do this. God did not kill Abel. God did not afflict Job.

The amazing thing is that the Master Weaver can create beauty at all in the midst of grief and pathos, that He can take that errant color woven into the tapestry of life by His enemy and turn it into a beautiful pattern.

The Master Weaver has done this since Cain killed Abel. His Church was founded on martyrs' blood. This is the heart of Romans 8:28 and Jesus' response to the disciples: "This happened so that the works of God might be displayed" (John 9:30 NIV). God did not cause the blindness; He healed it.

What makes the weaver a Master Weaver is His ability to take frail, mundane material in deleterious conditions and yet produce a masterpiece. That is the Master Weaver I know.

And that is the last time I will let Hallmark do my theology!

READ JOHN 9:1–12. WHAT WORK of God do you see Him doing in your life through this circumstance? What do you desire Him to do? Write out your prayer.

_____

_____

_____

_____

_____

_____

_____

_____

_____

_____

_____

_____

_____

_____

_____

_____

_____

_____

_____

_____

_____

_____

_____

_____

_____

_____

_____

_____

_____

_____

_____

_____

_____

_____

_____

_____

Schadenfreude

I HAVE ALWAYS THOUGHT THE concept of *schadenfreude*[5] unnatural, upside down. How could someone receive joy or comfort from the suffering of another? Sounds sinful to me.

Yet, I find I take comfort from Isaiah when he says, "In all their affliction, He was afflicted" (Isaiah 63:9 ESV).

It is a strange comfort to me that I am not alone in grief but that God suffers with me. If anyone knows suffering, it is He. I'm glad we're together.

AS YOU REFLECT ON ISAIAH 63:9, what comfort, if any, do you take in knowing He knows what you are going through? As described in Philippians 3:10–11, how can you relate to His suffering as well?

Do you know anyone going through the grieving process with whom you can relate?

_____

_____

_____

_____

_____

_____

_____

_____

_____

_____

---

5. *Schadenfreude* is one of those German ironies; it is the combination of the words *sorrow* and *joy*. It describes delight in another's misfortune.

_____

_____

_____

_____

_____

_____

_____

_____

_____

_____

_____

_____

_____

_____

_____

_____

_____

_____

_____

_____

_____

_____

_____

_____

_____

Psalm 126

Those who sow with tears
will reap with songs of joy.
Those who go out weeping,
carrying seed to sow,
will return with songs of joy,
carrying sheaves with them.

"The tears . . . streamed down, and I let them flow as freely as they
would, making of them a pillow for my heart. On them it rested."
—Augustine, "Confessions" IX, 12

HAVE YOU ALLOWED YOURSELF TIME to cry? Why or why not?
Find time this week to sit still in a quiet place alone and allow
your emotions to take over—sorrow, anger, joy, frustration. Allow
yourself the time and the freedom. Write your insights following
that experience.

_____

_____

_____

_____

_____

_____

_____

_____

_____

_____

_____

_____

_____

_____

_____

_____

_____

_____

_____

_____

_____

_____

_____

_____

_____

_____

_____

_____

_____

_____

_____

_____

_____

_____

_____

Fairness Doctrine

DAD ALWAYS WARNED ME, OF course, that life isn't fair. But he never thought to warn me of death. If life is unfair, death is even more so.

Of course, I know death will come . . . the whole death and taxes thing. But when? That's where the unfairness comes in.

The other day, I saw a man on the street. Old . . . no, ancient. His body barely functioning. He was searching for aluminum cans. Another passerby. Obese. Smoking.

But the bell tolled not for them. It tolled for Mom.

DOES LIFE SEEM UNFAIR? EXPLAIN. What aspects jump out at you as the most unfair?

_____

_____

_____

_____

_____

_____

_____

_____

_____

_____

_____

_____

_____

_____

_____

_____

_____

_____

_____

_____

_____

_____

_____

_____

_____

_____

_____

_____

_____

_____

_____

_____

_____

_____

_____

_____

_____

_____

_____

Demons

IT SEEMS TO ME THAT death brings to the forefront those demons within us that normally stay hidden. Fear, insecurity, inadequacy.

My wife, Christine, called yesterday and I didn't return her call immediately. A common occurrence in our busy lives. But this time it left her in a panic. Fear.

My struggle is with inadequacy. I preached the message at Mom's memorial service. And I've been told by countless friends and acquaintances what a wonderful message it was.

Still, my only conclusion on that message is that it failed. It wasn't enough. It did not adequately describe Mom or her Lord or minister to our family.

It was the most important message of my short life. It was vital for the healing of my wounded family and church. And it wasn't enough.

I wish I could do it over.

ARE THERE FEARS THAT HAUNT you during this time? Are you struggling with guilt or self-deprecation? What do you wish you could "do over"? As you list these things, give them to God. Ask for divine forgiveness if necessary. Forgive yourself if necessary.

_____

_____

_____

_____

_____

_____

_____

_____

_____

_____

_____

_____

_____

_____

_____

_____

_____

_____

_____

_____

_____

_____

_____

_____

_____

_____

_____

_____

_____

_____

_____

_____

_____

_____

_____

Treasure

"'Do not lay up for yourselves treasures on earth, where moth and rust destroy and where thieves break in and steal,'" taught the Lord.

"'But lay up for yourselves treasures in heaven. . . . For where your treasure is, there your heart will be also'" (Matthew 6:19–21 ESV).

I think I understand this now. Today, I have more treasure in heaven. That is where my heart is. She took it with her.

Jane Mann is a treasure.

How would you describe the treasure being stored in heaven for you? Does God want *you* to store up more? Write out what He's speaking to you.

_____

_____

_____

_____

_____

_____

_____

_____

_____

_____

_____

_____

_____

_____

A New Normal

Mother

WHAT IS IT THAT MAKES losing a mother so spiritually difficult? I'm seeing now that she was my first real connection to God.

She was the one who told me the stories, taught me the songs. Like God, she cared, nurtured, fed, clothed. She brought comfort, eased fears. She enjoyed life and made life enjoyable. Just like God.

Of course, Dad was like God, too. Only in a different way. He provided. He brought stability and dignity. He disciplined. Just like God.

Both provided excellent examples of the love of God, only differently. Mom's was more intimate.

I refuse to lose that intimacy with God. Mom wouldn't allow it.

DESCRIBE YOUR RELATIONSHIP WITH GOD. How has your experience with grief changed that relationship? What is your ultimate desire for that relationship? Does something need to change?

_____

_____

_____

_____

_____

_____

_____

_____

_____

_____

_____

_____

_____

_____

_____

_____

_____

_____

_____

_____

_____

_____

_____

_____

_____

_____

_____

_____

_____

_____

_____

_____

_____

_____

_____

Remember

"TIME HEALS ALL WOUNDS," WE are told. "Hold on to those precious memories of your mother." This is the advice I've been given. But they are at war with one another.

I do find that time has some healing properties. As days turn to weeks, each day is a little better. After all, God's mercies are new every morning (see Lamentations 3:23).

And the memories are wonderful. They make me smile, even if that smile is punctuated with a tear.

But here's the rub: I am already discovering that memories begin to fade with the passing of time. What did her voice sound like? How, again, did she smile exactly? What was that song she was always singing? I can't remember . . .

Time may indeed heal . . . but it is now my enemy. I want to remember. One of the judgments of God on the wicked is that they will be forgotten in the land of the living.

Mom is in Sheol now—the Old Testament "land of the dead"—and she is not cursed. Therefore I must remember.

I simply *must* remember.

SPEND SOME TIME "REMEMBERING" YOUR loved one today. Write down everything you remember: joyful memories, funny memories, and memories you want etched in stone.

_____

_____

_____

_____

_____

_____

Shine

Matthew 13:43 (NIV)

"'Then the righteous will shine
like the sun
in the kingdom
of their Father.'"

Mom shone!

MEDITATE ON THE PSALMS TODAY and write out one that particularly encouraged you.

_____

_____

_____

_____

_____

_____

_____

_____

_____

_____

_____

_____

_____

A New Normal

Shaded Gray

THE WAY I DESCRIBE IT is that I'm in a fog. Things are unclear, murky, surreal, as if I'm the hero in a Kafka story . . . things are happening with no seeming rhyme or reason.

My last thought before sleep finally comes is a thought about Mom. The first thought in the morning is the same. And if, by chance, I happen to awake in the watches of the night, well . . . I can only assume that my subconscious mind is continually processing Mom's death.

But since I can't come to an understanding of this, the fog rolls in. I've always loved a morning fog. At our family's cabin on the river, each morning comes with a thick, beautiful blanket of fog. But I don't like this fog. It's eerie.

A friend described it another way: "Everything will be gray for a while." A pretty good description. Life seems to have no vibrant, exciting contrasts of colors. Only grays in varying hues. So things lose their distinctness, their clarity. Like a fog. Spiritually, intellectually, emotionally.

I'm praying the sun will rise and burn it off. I like colors.

DESCRIBE THE FOG YOU ARE walking in today. Ask for God's help in navigating.

_____

_____

_____

_____

_____

_____

_____
_____
_____
_____
_____
_____
_____
_____
_____
_____
_____
_____
_____
_____
_____
_____
_____
_____
_____
_____
_____
_____
_____
_____
_____

Shadow of Death

"Yea, though I walk through the valley of the shadow of death, I will fear no evil. . . ." —Psalm 23:4 (KJV)

I'VE NOT GIVEN MUCH THOUGHT, until now, to the valley of the shadow of death. In my mind, the emphasis here has always been on the valley. A place. A dangerous place, a difficult circumstance, a desperate time.

But now I see the psalmist's remarks in another light. The emphasis is now, for me, on the *shadow* of death. Each of us has a shadow. A companion of silence following us, always on our heels. We look over our shoulder and see it close at hand. We cannot leave it behind. There are times, of course, when we can't see our shadow, but it is with us. The right lighting will once again reveal its presence.

Death is the shadow that pursues us. The valley is the place where it catches us.

For some, like Mother, the shadow finally catches us in our own bed. For others, perhaps, they meet their shadows in a more violent manner. The valleys may look different, but a valley is a valley.

"'Man who is born of a woman is few of days and full of trouble. He comes out like a flower and withers; he flees like a shadow and continues not.'"
—Job 14:1–2 (NIV)

The believer is not promised a life in which he will not meet his shadow. We all will. The benefit God gives the believer in the valley of the shadow of death is confidence—freedom from fear, light to dispel the darkness of the valley.

Living life "afraid of one's own shadow" is no life at all. So we continue through valleys, meadows, mountains, always with our silent companion trailing us.

But we don't fear it. Our God is a God of light, not shadows. Not murky, but of substance (Colossians 2:17). For our shadow has been defeated: "O death, where is thy sting? O grave, where is thy victory?" (1 Corinthians 15:55 KJV).

Though death may pursue us throughout our lives, so too does the love of God.

"Surely goodness and mercy shall follow me all the days of my
life: and I will dwell in the house of the Lord for ever."
—Psalm 23:6 (KJV)

"The shadow proves the sunshine."
—Switchfoot

DESCRIBE THE VALLEY YOU ARE walking through today. In specific terms describe the green pastures and still waters you are looking forward to. Pray Psalm 23 today.

_____

_____

_____

_____

_____

_____

_____

_____

_____

_____
_____
_____
_____
_____
_____
_____
_____
_____
_____
_____
_____
_____
_____
_____
_____
_____
_____
_____
_____
_____
_____
_____
_____
_____
_____

Florilegium

"THEREFORE, THERE IS NOW NO condemnation for those who are in Christ Jesus....And if the Spirit of him who raised Jesus from the dead is living in you, he who raised Christ from the dead will also give life to your mortal bodies because of his Spirit who lives in you."

—Romans 8:1, 11 (NIV)

"Then Jesus declared, 'I am the bread of life. Whoever comes to me will never go hungry, and whoever believes in me will never be thirsty. . . . For my Father's will is that everyone who looks to the Son and believes in him shall have eternal life, and I will raise them up at the last day.'"

—John 6:35, 40 (NIV)

"Brothers and sisters, we do not want you to be uninformed about those who sleep in death, so that you do not grieve like the rest of mankind, who have no hope. For we believe that Jesus died and rose again, and so we believe that God will bring with Jesus those who have fallen asleep in him. According to the Lord's word, we tell you that we who are still alive, who are left until the coming of the Lord, will certainly not precede those who have fallen asleep. For the Lord himself will come down from heaven, with a loud command, with the voice of the arch- angel and with the trumpet call of God, and the dead in Christ will rise first. After that, we who are still alive and are left will be caught up together with them in the clouds to meet the Lord in the air. And so we will be with the Lord forever. Therefore encourage one another with these words."

—1 Thessalonians 4:13–18 (NIV)

ARE YOU ENCOURAGED OR DISCOURAGED when you consider heaven? Describe how you picture heaven in your mind. (Suggested reading: *Heaven* by Randy Alcorn.[6])

_____

_____

_____

_____

_____

_____

_____

_____

_____

_____

_____

_____

_____

_____

_____

_____

_____

_____

_____

_____

_____

_____

_____

6.   Randy Alcorn, *Heaven* (Carol Stream, IL: Tyndale House Publishers, 2004).

A New Normal

Absurdity

NATURALISM SUGGESTS WE ARE CREATURES of chance—that time plus chance has produced the human race, that we exist in a closed and random system of life. Things happen for no apparent "reason." We will fulfill our days on the earth simply to become again part of the earth when life leaves our bodies. There's really no "absurdity" in this system of thought since, in reality, all of it is absurd and random.

How am I, a theist, to deal with absurdity? In my open system, "randomness" is replaced by "purpose," "chance" by "divine sovereignty." All well and good.

But how, then, am I to understand the absolute absurdity of Mom's death? From what I read, only 2 in 1 million Americans contract this disease each year. And of those who get it, it is fatal to only 30%. That is absurdity.

How can there be purpose in it? And if there *is* purpose, where is it?

Do I slide into an "unlucky naturalistic" reasoning? Do I blame Satan (and perhaps give him too much credit)? Do I blame God?

I struggle between these three options. And, in the meantime, I await the coroner's final report. I feel I should reach a conclusion before the coroner . . . I don't want him to be the final authority.

So, my question: Is God still God in the midst of absurdity? Despite absurdity? This is a mystery I ponder.

And I sense in my spirit that perhaps the answer comes, like many things with God, after time and patient waiting. But I *need* to know.

"'Truly, truly, I say to you, unless a grain of wheat falls into the earth and dies, it remains alone; but if it dies, it bears much fruit.'"
—John 12:24 (ESV)

What is the ultimate harvest of Mother's death? And how "involved" was God? It is a mystery . . . I'm searching.

"Truly, you are a God who hides himself, O God of Israel, the Savior."
—Isaiah 45:15 (ESV)

A religion which does not affirm that God is hidden is not true.

"Vere tu es Deus absconditus."
"Truly you are a hidden God."
—Pascal

WHAT DO YOU FIND MOST absurd about your present situation? What are the questions you need answered? Ask God for the answers—be patient as the answers come.

_____

_____

_____

_____

_____

_____

_____

_____

_____

_____

Blessed

Matthew 5:1–11 (NIV)

THERE ARE MANY THINGS IN this world that bring God's blessings upon us. Most are readily seen and easily understood:

- poor in spirit—theirs is the kingdom of heaven
- meek—they inherit the earth
- hunger and thirst for righteousness—they receive satisfaction
- merciful—they obtain mercy
- pure in heart—they see God
- peacemakers—they are called sons of God
- persecuted—theirs is the kingdom of heaven

These things I understand. Humility, gentleness, a desire for righteousness, mercy, purity, even being persecuted for one's faith—all of these character traits have intrinsic value in and of themselves. It seems only natural, then, since these are also godly traits, that the Lord would reward them.

But what is the intrinsic value of mourning? "'Blessed are those who mourn, for they will be comforted'" (v. 4). In what way does mourning "add to" life or to the kingdom of God? Why would God reward mourning?

Man is not "rewarded" for mourning any more than he is rewarded for breathing. Mourning is a part of each life. Jesus' apposition of mourning and comfort is given to heighten the stark contrast of God's kingdom versus the world's.

Jesus is showing that His kingdom is a complete upheaval of the world's system. It is opposite, upside down. In heaven's kingdom, the meek win. In heaven's kingdom, the humble are exalted.

In heaven's kingdom, the peacemakers—not the warriors—are powerful.

And so it is with the mourners. God promises us comfort. I am in mourning, but I have God's assurance of comfort. When? He does not say, but it will come.

I especially enjoy Luke's version of this statement: "Blessed are you who weep now, for you will laugh" (Luke 6:21 NIV).

I weep now. But I take heart from the very words of Jesus. I will laugh again.

It is a promise.

HAVE YOU COME TO A place where you can share your feelings? Have you come to a place where you have been able to mourn? Take time to pour out your heart to the Lord today.

_____

_____

_____

_____

_____

_____

_____

_____

_____

_____

_____

_____

The Bell Tolls

"ALL MANKIND IS OF ONE author, and is one volume; when one man dies, one chapter is not torn out of the book, but translated into a better language; and every chapter must be so translated; God employs several translators; some pieces are translated by age, some by sickness, some by war, some by justice; but God's hand is in every translation, and his hand shall bind up all our scattered leaves again for that library where every book shall lie open to one another. As therefore the bell that rings to a sermon calls not upon the preacher only, but upon the congregation to come, so this bell calls us all. . . .

"No man is an island, entire of itself; every man is a piece of the continent, a part of the main. If a clod be washed away by the sea, Europe is the less, as well as if a promontory were, as well as if a manor of thy friend's or of thine own were: any man's death diminishes me, because I am involved in mankind, and therefore never send to know for whom the bell tolls; it tolls for thee."

—John Donne, "For Whom the Bell Tolls"

IF YOU COULD WRITE THE last chapters in the story of your own life, what would they include? If you were planning your own funeral, who would be there? What would people say about you? Turn this into a prayer for the Lord to accomplish His goals and purposes in your life.

_____

_____

_____

_____

_____

_____

_____

_____

_____

_____

_____

_____

_____

_____

_____

_____

_____

_____

_____

_____

_____

_____

_____

_____

_____

_____

_____

In Vain?

"Vanity of vanities, says the Preacher, vanity of vanities! All is vanity."

—Ecclesiastes 1:2 (ESV)

IS IT VAIN TO LIVE a life in pursuit of God and His righteousness? Is it wrong to ask this question?

After all, as Solomon himself discovered, "The wise person has his eyes in his head, but the fool walks in darkness. And yet I perceived that the same event happens to all of them.... How the wise dies just like the fool! So I hated life, because what is done under the sun was grievous to me, for all is vanity and a striving after wind."

Grieving is certainly a grievous business!

Was Mom's life in vain, since she was not spared an untimely death? "For man does not know his time. Like fish that are taken in an evil net, and like birds that are caught in a snare, so the children of man are snared at an evil time, when it suddenly falls upon them."

Her life was not in vain. "The end of the matter; all has been heard. Fear God and keep his commandments, for this is the whole duty of man." There was no vanity—no chasing the wind—in the life of Jane Mann.

She feared God. She kept His commands. She fulfilled her duty.

She lived a life of reverence to God. She lived the totality of her life in subjection to His will.

And she did the same in death. "For everything there is a season ... a time to be born, and a time to die...."

And neither death, nor birth, need be in vain.

—Excerpts from Ecclesiastes 2, 3, 9, 12 (ESV)

WHERE DO YOU FIND THE most satisfaction in life? How can you measure your success in relation to that? What were the greatest successes of your loved one?

_____

_____

_____

_____

_____

_____

_____

_____

_____

_____

_____

_____

_____

_____

_____

_____

_____

_____

_____

_____

_____

_____

_____

_____

_____

Childlike Prayer

FOR A SECOND-GRADE CLASS ASSIGNMENT, my daughter, Reagan, wrote this letter to our family:

> dear the mann family.
>
> I hope we fell betr.
>
> I love you gise. We
>
> Are grate. I hope we
>
> Have fun.

At the bottom of the letter, in brown crayon, is a large wooden cross. Amen, Reagan. I hope we "fell betr" too.

WRITE YOUR OWN CHILDLIKE PRAYER to your Heavenly Daddy, Abba Father.

_____

_____

_____

_____

_____

_____

_____

_____

_____

_____

_____

_____

_____

_____

_____

_____

_____

_____

_____

_____

_____

_____

_____

_____

_____

_____

_____

_____

_____

_____

_____

_____

_____

_____

_____

_____

_____

_____

Strong as Death

"Set me as a seal upon your heart,
as a seal upon your arm,
for love is strong as death,
jealousy is fierce as the grave.
Its flashes are flashes of fire,
the very flame of the Lord.
Many waters cannot quench love,
neither can floods drown it.
If a man offered for love
all the wealth of his house,
he would be utterly despised."
—Song of Solomon 8:6–7(ESV)

IT IS INTERESTING TO ME how I remember, oftentimes, the circumstances surrounding my introduction to a "new" Scripture passage. I first became aware of this statement by Solomon's beloved as I planned my younger brother Mark and his wife Michelle's wedding. We used the Scripture in the ceremony. It is a wonderful description of love and very appropriate for describing the beginning of love.

Now, I read this again in a different light—at the end of love. And certainly, love is as strong as death. But my parents' love for one another is not removed by death, simply transformed.

With Mother gone, love has changed. But the seal on Dad's heart remains. The vehement flame still burns. The flood of tears has not drowned love. What will Dad do with this unrequited love? Will he continue on? Will he give up on life? Will he find joy again?

Will Dad discover where Mom ended and he began? Will he be able to "rediscover" himself? How does Ralph act, speak, live, and enjoy life without Jane, his constant companion for 43 years?

A great mystery—"'The two . . . become one flesh'" (Ephesians 5:31–32 NIV). Now must my father somehow extract himself? Must the one now become two again?

This is my dad's struggle. This is my struggle too, for I worry about my dad. I still think of Mom constantly. But now my selfishness is beginning to wear off. My thoughts of Mom don't linger as long on "my" loss but quickly move to Dad's loss. And what a terrible loss it is.

Misery is the word I use to describe it. I've thought much about the right description, and I've settled on *misery*. For I believe it encompasses the whole of Dad's suffering—emotional, physical, spiritual. He is miserable. Part of him has died. Yet he lives.

There are moments (many of them) during the day when I feel miserable. But my wife is still here. My kids bring me joy. My whole life is still ahead of me. And so, when I'm feeling miserable, I think of Dad and how *really* miserable he must be. I try to help but find I am more like Job's friends: "miserable comforters" (16:2 ESV).

I wish wise Solomon would have written that love is "stronger" than death. But he didn't. Death is strong. The grave is cruel. And human love, as powerful as it is, cannot overcome them.

Our only possible hope—Dad's only chance of overcoming—lies in divine love. For only God's love can overcome the grave. Only God's love can defeat death.

> "The Son of God . . . suffered unto the death, not that men might not suffer, but that their suffering might be like his."
> —George MacDonald, *Unspoken Sermons*[7]

---

7   George MacDonald, *Unspoken Sermons* (New York: Cosimo, Inc., 2007) 30.

A New Normal

"But rejoice insofar as you share Christ's sufferings, that you may also rejoice and be glad when his glory is revealed."
—1 Peter 4:13 (ESV)

". . . Can sadness be relieved, or can one only pass it by, very slowly? A day in the radiant sunlight and the sky's blue, in the shadow of a proud dark sail, over rustling waves, along new coastlines, wouldn't that help to get past sadness?—for a while, for that one day at least."
—Maria Dermout, *The Ten Thousand Things*[8]

COMPLETE THIS THOUGHT: LOVE IS. . . . Consider 1 John 4:9: God is love.

_____

_____

_____

_____

_____

_____

_____

_____

_____

_____

_____

_____

_____

_____

_____

_____

---

8. Maria Dermout, *The Ten Thousand Things* (Broadway, NY: The New York Review of Books, 2002) 97.

_____

_____

_____

_____

_____

_____

_____

_____

_____

_____

_____

_____

_____

_____

_____

_____

_____

_____

_____

_____

_____

_____

_____

_____

_____

This Shall Be a Sign?

(Psalm 18 ESV)

SINCE NOAH—AND MAYBE BEFORE—HUMANS HAVE sought numinous signs from God, revealing His hand in their circumstances. Both the Old and New Testaments are full of examples.

My clan and I are no different. Though we are "modern" men, we still seek signs for comfort, for guidance.

It was the night of Mom's admittance to the emergency room. Since I was not allowed to spend the night, I stayed and kept watch in her intensive care room until 2:00 a.m. I prayed much that evening. In my time of intercession and warfare, I was led to read Psalm 18. It is a beautiful psalm of deliverance:

> "The cords of death encompassed me;
> the torrents of destruction assailed me;
> the cords of Sheol entangled me;
> the snares of death confronted me."

Thus, facing death in that room, I, like the psalmist, prayed for deliverance:

> "In my distress I called upon the Lord;
> to my God I cried for help.
> from his temple he heard my voice,
> and my cry to him reached his ears."

In the psalm, God not only hears the call for help but responds. And His response is nothing short of breathtaking. The earth shakes with thunder. The dark night sky is split with bolts of lightning.

God descended into time and space through a storm and delivered the afflicted righteous.

August, up until then, had been hot and dry. In fact, little rain had fallen during the summer of 2005 in North Texas. But that night it rained. It rained hard with thunder and lightning. Was God responding just as He had done in the days of old? Had He heard our cries for help? Was this a sign of His deliverance?

The next morning, I shared the passage—and my thoughts on it—with Dad. He began to cry. He too, the night before, had prayed for rain. Apparently, Mom and Dad had always viewed rain from heaven as a sign of God's involvement in their lives. Whenever they had made major life decisions, he told me, God always seemed to show His approval by sending rain. So as Dad drove home from the hospital on the night of admittance, he'd asked God for a sign. "Please, let it rain."

I had my sign and renewed confidence in God's impending deliverance. After a week in the hospital, Mom was released. She died at home.

What about God's sign? Maybe I misinterpreted it. Maybe it was simply a summer Texas thunderstorm that popped up as two weather fronts collided, and maybe I just "happened" to read Psalm 18 that evening. And maybe I am simply part of that "wicked generation" who seeks signs because of a shallow faith (Luke 11:29 NIV). Maybe I have to "see" God move in order to believe in Him.

But signs *are* promised to those who believe in God. And the "wicked generation" seemed to be seeking signs out of disbelief. I believed. I was not looking for a sign. One appeared without my asking. And the Scripture passage simply helped me "interpret" it. So where is the promised deliverance? I have since read Psalm 18 many times over, looking for the answer. I have reached two conclusions on the matter.

The first deals with me. As I was the one led to Psalm 18 that night, the passage was for me. It was God's faithful promise for *my* deliverance. For shortly, I would be the one "in distress."

"For it is you who light my lamp;
the Lord my God lightens my darkness. . . .
This God—his way is perfect;
the word of the Lord proves true;
he is a shield for all those who take refuge in him."

God will deliver *me* from this darkness. He will be true. And He's given me a sign.

The second deals with Mom—after all, I wasn't praying for me, but her. She too has been delivered.

"He rescued me from my strong enemy. . . .
He brought me out into a broad place;
he rescued me, because he delighted in me."

Truly, Mom has been delivered. The strong enemies—sickness and death—have been destroyed by a resurrection. A wonderful place with God. Why? Because He delights in her. Who wouldn't?

This brings us back to "signs." The day before the funeral, we awoke to find above Mom's house the most beautiful rainbow I have ever seen. The colors were crystal clear, distinct. You could follow it from one end to the other. And, as if that weren't enough, it was a double rainbow. Two rainbows, stacked on top of each other in the Texas sky.

God called the rainbow a "sign" to Noah. It was a sign of His deliverance. Though tragedy had struck, God was with this clan and brought them through the flood. He had protected them, delivered them.

Further, on the way home from Mom's interment, a light shower fell on our caravan. That night, at the memorial service, God sent a torrential downpour!

And so, I am thankful for the signs—perhaps now rightly interpreted—of God's love. And I will continue to keep an eye open for God's hand in my family's life.

"I love you, O Lord, my strength. . . .

I call upon the Lord, who is worthy to be praised,

and I am saved from my enemies."

WRITE DOWN YOUR FAVORITE VERSE(S) in Psalm 18. Write a prayer using these verses in relation to your personal situation.

_____

_____

_____

_____

_____

_____

_____

_____

_____

_____

_____

_____

_____

_____

Trumped

People say some pretty dumb things to grieving friends. One such email read, "Jim, I'm sorry to hear about your loss—my mother has been sick recently, and I know just what you are going through." Really?

Another common response is what I call the "Grief Trump." It can be as simple as someone telling you that they too lost a loved one, or as complex as telling how their loss was worse than yours.

In the grieving process, you have to make a decision early on not to take offense at such well-meant but misguided statements.

The reality is that no one really knows "how" to grieve or how to help others who are grieving. And since we feel that we must say something, what we say is often not helpful.

Hurricane Katrina struck three weeks after Mom's death. My grief has been trumped. I know that all grief is unique and that one person's grief is not technically "worse" than someone else's. However, I think it is one thing to lose a mother in her sleep and quite another to have your mother swept away in a deluge of water.

And so my family has thrown itself into relief efforts. Why? Does it help us take our minds off of Mom's death? Is it because we can finally relate to those who have lost?

I'm not sure. But my prayer is that, somehow, the empathy I feel and the service I render will also help me.

The fellowship of Christ's suffering now includes more than my family. It is a large community. I'm praying this fellowship leads also to the power of His Resurrection.

MINISTERING TO OTHERS CAN QUITE often ease our pain by taking our focus off ourselves. Consider areas where you might serve or minister to those in need. Make a decision today to find someone in need and reach out to them.

_____

_____

_____

_____

_____

_____

_____

_____

_____

_____

_____

_____

_____

_____

_____

_____

_____

_____

_____

_____

_____

_____

_____

_____

_____

_____

_____

_____

_____

_____

_____

_____

_____

_____

_____

_____

_____

_____

_____

_____

_____

_____

_____

_____

_____

_____

_____

_____

_____

_____

_____

Praises

Throughout the days following Mom's death, many praises were sung and spoken. In conversations. At the interment. At the memorial service. We spoke freely—often through tears—of God's goodness despite the circumstances.

But the most powerful praises to God weren't spoken by me or by the "clergy." They came from Dad.

I will never forget. Mom had already died when Dad arrived at the house. As she lay "sleeping" in her bed, only Dad and I were present in the room with her body. We were both crying. Then Dad began to speak . . . to cry out to God. What would he say? Would he ask "Why?" Would he exhibit anger in the loss of his best friend?

Praises! Dad began to praise the Lord. Praises that she was with God. Praises for her wonderful life. Praises to the living God for His wonderful, mysterious plans.

Amazing! Nothing short of amazing. What a godly man. What composure. What depth of spirit. What leadership.

What a great man! What a great God—deserving the praises He receives.

I choose to imitate them both.

TAKE A MOMENT TO WRITE praises to the Lord. Use the Psalms as a reference if needed.

_____

_____

_____

_____

_____

_____

_____

_____

_____

_____

_____

_____

_____

_____

_____

_____

_____

_____

_____

_____

_____

_____

_____

_____

_____

_____

_____

_____

_____

_____

_____

_____

_____

_____

_____

Emotional Lottery

I'M NOT AN UNEMOTIONAL CREATURE, but I've never experienced emotions quite like this. It seems that grief is like a fire. I am like a pot of water placed on the fire. What bubble to the surface are emotions I never knew were there.

What is strange is the wide range of emotions that bubbles up. It's like one of those machines used to determine lottery numbers. The numbered ping-pong balls fly around in a whirlwind until one is sucked into the pneumatic tube. The spokesmodel pulls it out, looks at it, and reads the number to the audience: "23. . . 47 . . . 15. . . 31."

My emotions are similar. I go through the day and, at different times and circumstances, an emotional ping-pong ball is called: anger . . . frustration . . . indecision . . . sorrow.

I never know what will pop up. Or when. Very strange . . . the emotional toll it takes is taxing. The suspense is killing me. What will surface today?

IDENTIFY THE EMOTIONS YOU ARE experiencing in this difficult time. What are the thoughts and feelings behind them? Are you responding more from your heart or your head? Ask the Lord to help and heal your emotions.

_____

_____

_____

_____

_____

_____

Thy Will Be Done

I have alluded to the fact that one of my struggles, as an armchair theologian, is theological in nature.

If I were, say, a Calvinist, I would not have such a problem. Mom's death could simply be chalked up as "God's mysterious will." Still in pain, I would simply be forced to move on, as if this were part of a preordained, divinely inspired plan beyond my mortal comprehension. Perhaps, at this point, I would be forced to deal with anger toward God and His judgments, but I would move forward. After all, though mysterious, the divine will is both good and just. *Deo volente.*

However, I do not fully embrace such theology. Coming from the background of a more Arminian perspective, I must reach some conclusions. It is interesting that such an event leads one to reevaluate literally everything. . . .

And so I have engaged in my own weak theodicy. It is not God's fault. And though, technically, it can be seen as God's "will" that Mom died, it was not His perfect will "as it is in heaven" (Matthew 6:10).

My mind and heart have reached an armistice in this battle.

But I come to another layer of thinking that I have been trying to avoid. It raises specters that haunt my entire theological framework. C. S. Lewis points out that error begets error . . . so I go back to the beginning and reexamine, to see if there is error.

The thinking goes like this: God has given me authority in the spiritual realm. It is limited, of course, and wholly unearned. But it is real. A corollary to this is the belief that prayer works and can change circumstances.

Now, I do not believe this places too much emphasis on me and my station in either the universe or God's plan. But in humility, I believe it to be true and biblical.

With these conclusions, my dilemma arises: A + B = C.

A = God has given me some authority.
B = My will, my desire, was for Mom's healing.

Following this logic, C should have been the sum of the two: Mom's full recovery.

Or, stated another way:

A = Prayer changes things.
B = I prayed and fasted for Mom's healing.
C = Mom's full recovery would be seen.

But, of course, in both equations, "C" was that Mother died. So, I must reevaluate "A" and "B."

"A" seems to remain constant, as both lie with God. He has given believers authority, and He has promised power in prayer.

So the error must logically lie in "B." Maybe I didn't *use* my authority to the fullest, too timid, too "unenlightened." Maybe I didn't pray hard enough, fast long enough, get enough support from other "pray-ers."

This naturally leads to guilt—personal guilt—as if Mom's death were partially my fault. It leads to blame. When I asked the church to fast with me, did they? How many?

I am working through these questions, and my theology. I do not desire to go through life guilt-ridden, nor do I want to hold anything against my congregation.

Perhaps the equation itself is not as logical as I think. Perhaps "C" is much more complex than I believe. And maybe, just maybe, my theodicy is correct.

"Your will be done on earth as it is in heaven." After all, this wasn't a promise or a command, but a prayer, a petition. And a reality I'm forced to concede is that no matter what authority or level of prayer, it doesn't always work that way on this fallen planet.

ALTHOUGH THE FINAL ANSWER TO this question may never be given this side of heaven, consider the sovereignty of God. How do you account for the painful things we endure in our life?

_____

_____

_____

_____

_____

_____

_____

_____

_____

_____

_____

_____

_____

_____

_____

_____

_____

_____

Get on with Life

I KNOW THAT, ULTIMATELY, THIS is the conclusion one must reach at the end of grief: time to get on with life. I say "at the end" of grief, although I now understand that grief has no terminus. Probably it should read "at the ultimate embracing of grief."

Dad has even made this determination, which sounded strange coming from his lips. But get on with life?

> "These all died in faith, not having received the things promised, but having seen them and greeted them from afar, and having acknowledged that they were strangers and exiles on the earth. For people who speak thus make it clear that they are seeking a homeland. . . . They desire a better country, that is, a heavenly one. . . ."
>
> —Hebrews 11:13–16 (ESV)

Grief, I think, is a short (or long) rest stop on the journey home. It is a chance to remember from whence we have come. It is a chance to recalibrate directions. And as such, grief itself is an encouragement to continue on.

> "Therefore, since we are surrounded by so great a cloud of witnesses, . . . let us run with endurance the race that is set before us, looking to Jesus. . . ."
>
> —Hebrews 12:1–2 (ESV)

The journey must continue. We must, after all, "get on with life." For those of us who remain, our work is not yet complete.

"'The only wisdom' for one 'haunted with the scent of unseen
roses, is work.'"
—C. S. Lewis quoting George MacDonald, *The Problem of Pain*[9]

AS WE RUN THIS RACE called life, what are some obstacles we must
face? What are the greatest obstacles you face now? How does having
the "great cloud of witnesses" encourage you in this race? Write a
prayer for God's grace and mercy as you "get back on track."

_____

_____

_____

_____

_____

_____

_____

_____

_____

_____

_____

_____

_____

_____

_____

_____

_____

9.   C. S. Lewis, *The Problem of Pain: How Human Suffering Raises Almost Intoler-
     able Intellectual Problems* (New York: Collier Books, MacMillan Publishing
     House, 1962).

On Heaven

HEAVEN IS "THAT SOMETHING YOU were born desiring, and which, beneath the flux of other desires and in all the momentary silences between the louder passions, night and day, year by year, from childhood to old age, you are looking for, watching for, listening for. You have never had it. All the things that have ever deeply possessed your soul have been but hints of it—tantalizing glimpses, promises never quite fulfilled; echoes that died away just as they caught your ear. But if it should really become manifest—if there ever came an echo that did not die away but swelled into the sound itself—you would know it. Beyond all possibility of doubt you would say, 'Here at last is the thing I was made for.' We cannot tell each other about it. It is the secret signature of each soul, the incommunicable and unappeasable want, the thing we desired before we met our wives or made our friends or chose our work, and which we shall still desire on our deathbeds, when the mind no longer knows wife or friend or work. While we are, this is. If we lose this, we lose all."

". . . The mould in which a key is made would be a strange thing, if you had never seen a key: and the key itself a strange thing if you had never seen a lock. Your soul has a curious shape because it is a hollow made to fit a particular swelling in the infinite contours of the Divine substance, or a key to unlock one of the doors in the house with many mansions."

—C. S. Lewis, *The Problem of Pain*[10]

---

10. See note 9.

AS YOU CONSIDER HEAVEN, WHAT excites you most? What scares you most? What are you most unsure about? Write out all your thoughts concerning this wonderful and mysterious place.

_____

_____

_____

_____

_____

_____

_____

_____

_____

_____

_____

_____

_____

_____

_____

_____

_____

_____

_____

_____

_____

_____

_____

_____

_____

_____

_____

_____

_____

_____

_____

_____

_____

_____

_____

_____

_____

_____

_____

_____

_____

_____

_____

_____

_____

_____

_____

_____

_____

_____

On Eternity

"For this is what the high and exalted One says—he who lives
forever. . . ."
—Isaiah 57:15 (NIV)

"He has made everything beautiful in its time. He has also set
eternity in the human heart; yet no one can fathom what God
has done from beginning to end."
—Ecclesiastes 3:11 (NIV)

"But do not forget this one thing, dear friends: With the Lord
a day is like a thousand years, and a thousand years are like a day."
—2 Peter 3:8 (NIV)

TIME IS A PART OF life. Humans are constrained by beginnings and
ends. But the Lofty One who lives forever is not so constrained.
Over and over in the book of Hebrews, we see that God is in
the "eternal now." There is no beginning or end with God. He is
outside our understanding of time.

God's description of Himself as the Alpha and Omega should
therefore be properly viewed as acquiescence. God—though above
and beyond human timekeeping—has nevertheless chosen to in-
volve Himself in time and space. He has willingly put the restraints
of time—by which He is not normally bound—upon Himself. This
is concession. Like Revelation or Incarnation, God moves within
our sphere and reasoning to make Himself known. Creation, the
Exodus, the Crucifixion, the Resurrection—all of these occurred

in time and space, in human history. The consummation will occur at a fixed point in time in the future.

In the divine perspective, this is all taking place "now." Because God is eternal and beyond time, God is outside its confines.

If you were to look at time and history as linear—as we do in the West—you would have two fixed points at either end of a line. On the one end is the point of "beginning." On the other extreme is the point of "end." In between the two are births and deaths, wars and revolutions, the rise and fall of empires, and you.

And if for a moment you were allowed to "step away" from time, your perspective would change. As you step back from the timeline, you can now see "beginning" and "end" at the same moment. As you step back farther, the distance between the two points seems to shorten even more. If you could step back far enough, the timeline itself would become a dot on the page.

Time is a human construct. As such, our timeline is appropriately labeled "Human History." And God is not human. His otherness is what removes Him from time and gives Him the perspective just described. He may move in human history, but He is not bound to it. He is eternal. This is eternity.

This same eternity has been set in human hearts as well. But not now. We are in the midst of time, in the middle of history. We must go through our beginnings and ends.

And when the end of our personal history arrives, eternity begins. Perhaps this is not the best way to describe it, as *eternity* by definition can have no beginning. Maybe, at the end, eternity *continues* for us.

Our lives are hidden in Christ. And "in Him," eternity has been set in our hearts. Eternity is not merely the lengthening or extension of time. Rather, eternity is the removal of the constraints of time. We are less "taken into" eternity and more "delivered from" time.

At Mother's "end," as she was embraced by God, this became her reality. In heaven, in God's presence, there is no sorrow. No loss. No waiting. No anticipation for loved ones. She has been delivered from time. She is in the "eternal now." In a moment there will be reunion, but even that is not true, as "moments" describe time. Though she may be conscious of absence from Dad, she must, somehow, in the "eternal now," also be conscious of his presence.

> "... And God himself will be with them and be their God.
> 'He will wipe every tear from their eyes. There will be no
> more death' or mourning or crying or pain, for the old order of
> things has passed away."
> —Revelation 21:3–4 (NIV)

No sorrow. No loss. No waiting. No anticipation. This is *our* lot—those of us who remain, those still shackled by time.

But eternity is set in our hearts. Soon, we too will be delivered from the old order and embraced by God in His "eternal now."

It's the waiting that is hard.

IF YOU WERE IN CONTROL of the eternal clock, would you speed things up or slow things down? If you had to be stuck in one moment in time, when and where would it be?

_____

_____

_____

_____

_____

_____

Crossing the Bar

Sunset and evening star,
And one clear call for me!
And may there be no moaning of the bar,
When I put out to sea,

But such a tide as moving seems asleep,
Too full for sound and foam,
When that which drew from out the boundless deep
Turns again home.

Twilight and evening bell,
And after that the dark!
And may there be no sadness of farewell,
When I embark;

For tho' from out our bourne of Time and Place
The flood may bear me far,
I hope to see my Pilot face to face
When I have cross'd the bar.

—Alfred, Lord Tennyson

WHAT ARE SOME THINGS YOU desire to ask of your "Pilot" when you "cross the bar"?

_____

_____

_____

_____

A New Normal

Ich Glaube an Gott

KARL BARTH, THE GREAT GERMAN theologian, opposer of Hitler, and leader of the "Confessing Church," left his prestigious position at the University of Bonn as the Nazis rose to power. He left Germany for Switzerland.

When the war ended, Barth was invited back to be a professor at Bonn. Only now, the university lay in ruins. He held class amid the rubble.

When he began his first class on theology after the war, he began with these words: "*Ich glaube an Gott. . . .*"— "I believe in God. . . ."[11]

Despite the war, despite the destruction of life and property, despite the murder of millions of Jews, despite his own personal persecution—in the face of sin and death—"*Ich glaube an Gott.*" How appropriate.

I find myself in the same position in my own life. In the face of sin—I believe in God. In the face of death—I believe in God.

"Immediately the boy's father exclaimed, 'I do believe; help me overcome my unbelief!'"

—Mark 9:24 (NIV)

Ich glaube an Gott. What else can I do?

---

11. Foy Valentine, *Whatsoever Things Are Lovely* (Scriptum Publishing House, 2004) 158.

IN THE MIDST OF YOUR current trials, write your own personal statement of faith here.

_____

_____

_____

_____

_____

_____

_____

_____

_____

_____

_____

_____

_____

_____

_____

_____

_____

_____

_____

_____

_____

_____

_____

_____

_____

_____

_____

_____

_____

_____

_____

_____

_____

_____

_____

_____

_____

_____

_____

_____

_____

_____

_____

_____

_____

_____

_____

_____

_____

_____

_____

_____

_____

Sorrow, Joy, and Hope

"NOR DO WE KNOW HOW much of the pleasures even of life we owe to the intermingled sorrows. Joy cannot unfold the deepest truths, although the deepest truth must be deepest joy. Cometh white-robed Sorrow, stooping and wan, and flingeth wide the doors she may not enter. Almost we linger with Sorrow for very love."

—George MacDonald,
Phantastes[12]

"'Truly, truly, I say to you, you will weep and lament, but the world will rejoice. You will be sorrowful, but your sorrow will turn into joy. When a woman is giving birth, she has sorrow because her hour has come, but when she has delivered the baby, she no longer remembers the anguish, for joy that a human being has been born into the world.'"

—John 16:20–21 (ESV)

"It is the nature of grace always to fill spaces that have been empty."

—Goethe

---

12. George MacDonald, *Phantastes* (London: Smith, Elder, and Co., 1858) 116.

HOW CAN PAIN AND SORROW bring growth in your own life? How can you now comfort someone in a way you could not have several months ago?

_____

_____

_____

_____

_____

_____

_____

_____

_____

_____

_____

_____

_____

_____

_____

_____

_____

_____

_____

_____

_____

_____

_____

_____

_____

Mom's Birthday

THE FIRST THOUGHT AS COBWEBS cleared this morning, October 31, was "It is Mom's birthday." As I look at my daily schedule on my palm pilot, there's a note: "Mom's Birthday." And when I get to my office, there is a "Birthday" reminder on my calendar—like I need to be reminded.

I've always loved Halloween. We had a blast in costumes and trick-or-treating as kids. And though there was always a little creepiness in our celebration, we never really focused on death. After all, it was Mom's birthday . . . we celebrated her life! She would be 65 today!

As I thought about this, I was reminded that October 31 is also All Saint's Day. What a great day to remember Mom!

"We are surrounded by such a great cloud of witnesses. . . ."
—Hebrews 12:1 (NIV)

"That the God of our Lord Jesus Christ, the Father of glory, may give unto you the spirit of wisdom and revelation in the knowledge of him: The eyes of your understanding being enlightened; that ye may know what is the hope of his calling, and what the riches of the glory of his inheritance in the saints."
—Ephesians 1:17–18 (KJV)

This designation of believers as "saints," of course, is interesting. The Greek *hagios* describes holiness, especially in the sense of being "set apart" for the holy purposes of God. In this sense, all Christians are saints—but some can be saintlier than others.

Mother was certainly set apart to make a difference. And part of her calling was the "setting apart" of others. She spent 43 years making Dad's dreams come true—taking a good man and making him great, setting him apart for God's holy purposes.

She spent 35 years doing the same for me—perhaps not making me great but preparing me for greatness.

And such is God's inheritance in the saints. God's true saints, these "saintlier" saints, like Mom, make a difference, leave a mark, produce a legacy—"the hope of his calling."

As a saint myself, such should be my striving in life. First, to be holy and set apart for God's purposes in my life. Second, to strive, like Mom, to help set others apart—to prepare them for greatness. And third, to continue Mom's legacy as a saint—the "hope of his calling."

WRITE OUT EPHESIANS 1:17–18 AND change "you" to "me." In light of this great power given to you, how are you using it?

_____

_____

_____

_____

_____

_____

_____

_____

_____

_____

_____

_____

_____

_____

_____

_____

_____

_____

_____

_____

_____

_____

_____

_____

_____

_____

_____

_____

_____

_____

_____

_____

_____

_____

_____

_____

_____

_____

_____

On Love

$$\text{\textit{On Love}}$$

"I KNEW NOW, THAT IT is by loving, and not by being loved, that one can come nearest the soul of another; yea, that, where two love, it is the loving of each other, and not the being beloved by each other, that originates and perfects and assures their blessedness. I knew that love gives to him that loveth, power over any soul beloved, even if that soul know him not, bringing him inwardly close to that spirit; a power that cannot be but for good; for in proportion as selfishness intrudes, the love ceases, and the power which springs therefrom dies. Yet all love will, one day, meet with its return. All true love will, one day, behold its own image in the eyes of the beloved, and be humbly glad. This is possible in the realms of lofty Death."

—George MacDonald, *Phantastes*[13]

EXPLAIN WHAT IT MEANS TO be loved unconditionally. Can anyone but God do this? Compare the feelings of "loving" versus "being loved." Which is more important to you, to God? What do you need the most now?

_____

_____

_____

_____

_____

_____

_____

13. George MacDonald, *Phantastes* (London: Smith, Elder, and Co., 1858) 316.

_____

_____

_____

_____

_____

_____

_____

_____

_____

_____

_____

_____

_____

_____

_____

_____

_____

_____

_____

_____

_____

_____

_____

_____

_____

Crash

THE SLOW PROCESS OF ENTROPY has ground to a halt; the crash
of implosion now envelops me.

Enemies. Sabeans, Chaldeans, a mighty wind. Debris and shrap-
nel fly—where's my offense, where's my sin? Skin for skin?!

Surrounded by people, but no one's near but miserable coun-
selors—I grope, but can't find you here.

Where are you? The church house, the forest, the ocean's beach?
Are you truly hidden? Are you within reach?

So my search continues, my search continues.

I imagine your embrace and the comfort it gives when we meet
face to face, and I know my Redeemer lives.

And who can stand against You? Who can stand against You?

—from the book of Job

EXPRESS YOUR THOUGHTS OF LONELINESS to the Lord. Turn this
into a prayer for His unconditional love. Explain how this love
encourages you.

_____

_____

_____

_____

_____

_____

_____

_____

_____

In

||||||||||||||||||||||||||||||||||||||||||||||||||||||||||||||||||||||||||||||||||||||||||||||||||||||||

"BEFORE LONG, THE WORLD WILL not see me anymore, but you will see me. Because I live, you also will live. On that day you will realize that I am in my Father, and you are in me, and I am in you."

—John 14:19–20 (NIV)

"In-ness is a most fundamental expression of existence. It is through being in Christ Who lives that we live. That part of you in your mother did not die, for she is not dead. Christ lives, and she lives in Him. That part of you in her lives closer to Him than ever before."

—A Friend

WHAT ENCOURAGEMENT DO YOU FIND in knowing that Jesus is "in you" and you are "in Him"? How can you relate to Him in a new way with this revelation? Write a prayer keeping this in mind.

_____

_____

_____

_____

_____

_____

_____

_____

_____

_____

The Setting Sun

"I've got a wound that doesn't heal,
Burning out again,
Burning out again.

I'm not sure which of me is real.
And I'm alone again,
Burning out again.

My hope runs underneath it all,
The day that I'll be home.

It won't be long. I belong
Somewhere past this setting sun,

Finally free, finally strong
Somewhere back where I belong.

They're selling shares of me again,
But I'm not buying it.
I'm not buying it.

My wound goes deeper than the skin.
There's no hiding it,
So I'm not trying it.

My hope runs underneath it all,
The day that I'll be home,

Finally back where we belong.
Finally free.
It's gonna take you to the setting sun.

Let the weak say I am strong,
And it won't be long.
Let the right say I was wrong,
And it won't be long.

Let us find where we belong
Beyond this setting sun."

—Switchfoot

Choose a song that has been particularly encouraging to you during your grief and write it out. Use it as a prayer to write out to the Father.

_____

_____

_____

_____

_____

_____

_____

_____

_____

_____

_____

_____

Scars

"'Look at my hands and my feet. It is I myself! Touch
me and see; a ghost does not have flesh and bones, as
you see I have.' When he had said this, he showed them
his hands and feet."

—Luke 24:39–40 (NIV)

"Then I saw a Lamb, looking as if it had been slain,
standing at the center of the throne, encircled by the
four living creatures and the elders. . . ."

—Revelation 5:6 (NIV)

IT IS INTERESTING AND IRONIC that the glorification of Christ did
not erase the scars. At the Resurrection, Jesus will return. Glori-
fied. With scars.

When Thomas and the disciples encountered the risen Lord,
their excitement must have been overwhelming. But the joy of the
reunion could not erase the fact that three days earlier they had
witnessed the terrible Crucifixion. They were scarred themselves.

And no matter what joy comes after pain, be it resurrection or
reunion, the scars remain throughout life. Sure, they heal. They
no longer cause so much pain. Time passes, and they are less
noticeable. But they are still there . . . and always will be . . . to
remind us of loss.

This must be a good thing—part of God's design. For, other-
wise, the resurrected Lord would have shown up without scars.
The Lamb would not have shown signs of sacrifice. But He did,
and He does.

117

In both cases—in Jerusalem and in heaven—the scars are no longer focal points for life. They were used by the Lord to prove His identify as the Suffering Servant. In heaven, it will be similar with us. Sure, these scars are part of who we are and our own life story, but they serve only to identify us and no longer define us.

> "There is something beautiful about all scars of whatever nature. A scar always means the hurt is over, the wound is closed and healed, done with."
> —Harry Crews[14]

WHAT IS YOUR MOST PAINFUL scar? Do you feel that whenever you meet someone, the scar is all they see? Does this journal entry change your perspective on scars? How?

_____

_____

_____

_____

_____

_____

_____

_____

_____

_____

_____

_____

---

14. Harry Crews, *Scar Lover* (New York: Touchstone, 1992) 142.

A New Normal

_____
_____
_____
_____
_____
_____
_____
_____
_____
_____
_____
_____
_____
_____
_____
_____
_____
_____
_____
_____
_____
_____
_____
_____
_____
_____
_____
_____

Final Thoughts

AS THIS TIME OF JOURNALING through your grief comes to a close, write out your final thoughts. Sum up what you have learned, as a legacy of sorts for those who will follow after you. How might your journal be used to encourage others on their own personal journey?

_____

_____

_____

_____

_____

_____

_____

_____

_____

_____

_____

_____

_____

_____

_____

_____

_____

_____

_____

_____

A New Normal

Afterword

Like me, you'll probably never "finish" the grieving process. But the process will change and, I think, become easier—even joyful. Let the Lord work in your life, and take courage.

> "Restore our fortunes, Lord,
> like streams in the Negev.
> Those who sow with tears
> will reap with songs of joy.
> Those who go out weeping,
> carrying seed to sow,
> will return with songs of joy,
> carrying sheaves with them."
> —Psalm 126:4–6 (NIV)

For more information about
Jim Mann
&
A New Normal
please visit:

DrJimMann.com
info@drjimmann.com

For more information about
AMBASSADOR INTERNATIONAL
please visit:

www.ambassador-international.com
@AmbassadorIntl
www.facebook.com/AmbassadorIntl